SIERRA CLUB EXHIBIT FORMAT SERIES

Winner of the Carey-Thomas Award in 1964
    for the best achievement in creative publishing in the United States

EDITED BY DAVID BROWER

for mom and dad

    on this Christmas-come-early, 1971.

    Here is New York in her most

    rare moments.

    Our love is with you both,

        Ian + Anne

Central Park Country

From the Professional Papers
of Frederick Law Olmsted, Sr.

The population of your city, increasing with such prodigious rapidity; your sultry summers, and the corrupt atmosphere generated in hot and crowded streets, make it a cause of regret that in laying out New York, no preparation was made, while it was yet practicable, for a range of parks and public gardens along the central part of the island or elsewhere, to remain perpetually for the refreshment and recreation of the citizens during the torrid heats of the warm season. There are yet unoccupied lands on the island which might, I suppose, be procured for the purpose, and which, on account of their rocky and uneven surfaces, might be laid out into surpassingly beautiful pleasure-grounds; but while we are discussing the subject the advancing population of the city is sweeping over them and covering them from our reach. [William Cullen Bryant in the Evening Post, 1845, quoted p. 23.]

Central Park, the artifact of a thousand hands,
has the inevitability of a natural force.

Man, with imagination and confidence, has created in the center of
Manhattan an island within an island. Yet it is no oasis, no secluded
Arcadia, sheltered from the hectic concrete and glass jungle surrounding
it; the park is the living core around which the city organizes and by
which it is nourished.

It is as if all the parallel furrows of those endless streets and those interminably stretched avenues had to pass through the park to gain vitality, strength, and meaning. As if the contrived pattern of their course came here to learn about whim and diversity.

Like any kingdom, the park has its own local ceremonies, its sacred animals, its holy places. Here the New Yorker comes, and through rites, games, and parades, through pilgrimages to the meadows and beside the ponds, exorcises his fears; he pursues the quest of wonder through new patterns; he hears once again, if ever so faintly, the world's music and his own.

Photographs by NANCY *and* RETTA JOHNSTON

Introduction by MARIANNE MOORE

CENTRAL PARK COUNTRY

SIERRA CLUB

A TUNE WITHIN US

Text by MIREILLE JOHNSTON

edited, with a foreword, by DAVID BROWER

SAN FRANCISCO   NEW YORK   LONDON

The Sierra Club, founded in 1892 by John Muir, has devoted itself to the study and protection of scenic resources and wild places around the world. Sierra Club publications are part of the nonprofit effort the club carries on as a public trust. The club is affiliated with the International Union for Conservation, the National Resources Council of America, the Conservation Foundation, and the Federation of Western Outdoor Clubs. There are chapters in California, the Pacific Northwest, the Great Basin, the Southwest, the Great Lakes region, on the Atlantic Seaboard, Hawaii, and Alaska. Participation is invited in the program to enjoy and preserve wilderness, wildlife, forests, and streams. *Main office: Mills Tower, San Francisco. Other offices: 15 E. 53rd. St., New York; 235 Massachusetts Ave., NE, Washington D.C.; 6 Langley St., London W.C.2; 427 West 5th St., Los Angeles; and in Seattle, Washington, and Albuquerque, New Mexico.*

We gratefully acknowledge permission to reprint material from Frederick Law Olmsted, Jr. and Theodora Kimball (eds.), Forty Years of Landscape Architecture, Being the Professional Papers of Frederick Law Olmsted, Senior. Volume II: Central Park, as a Work of Art and as a Great Municipal Enterprise, 1853-1895. New York and London: G. P. Putnam's Sons, The Knickerbocker Press, © 1928.

Publisher's Note: The book is set in Centaur and Arrighi by Mackenzie & Harris, Inc., San Francisco. It was lithographed on Capital Star Sapphire by Barnes Press, New York City, and bound in Columbia Mills Bradford linen by A. Horowitz & Son, Clifton, New Jersey. The design is by David Brower.

For Tom

CONTENTS

NINETY-THREE COLOR PLATES

FOREWORD

There are many Central Parks and Mireille Johnston's is one of the most beautiful of all. Her husband's sisters, Retta and Nancy Johnston, have found and photographed the same beauty and the reflection of it in people. It becomes E. B. White's ". . . loveliest town of all, where the houses were white and high and the elm trees were green and higher than the houses, where the front yards were wide and pleasant and the back yards were bushy and worth finding out about, where the streets sloped down to the stream and the stream flowed quietly under the bridge, where the lawns ended in orchards and the orchards ended in the fields and the fields ended in pastures and the pastures climbed the hill and disappeared over the top toward the wonderful wide sky . . ."

Central Park's bordering hills are steeper and its sky is not quite so wide. There will be more people near by if you, like Stuart Little, stop for a drink of sarsaparilla. Otherwise, Central Park could well be Manhattan's loveliest town of all.

It can be many other things, too. Its shrubs and trees can harbor crime. It can be the darkest part of a city of night. It can be a temptation to those who would put its open land on the tax rolls. It could tempt others, whatever the cost in visual rights, to close this land with warehouses, parking lots, fire and police stations, extensions of museums and restaurants, or to try out new kinds of motorized vehicles. It can even remain what Frederick Law Olmsted [1822-1903], father of American landscape architecture, wanted it to be.

But none of these potentials is quite up to what the Johnstons see in Central Park and what their book seeks to reveal. Mrs. Johnston, in the four movements of her text, is sensitive as only a person from faraway can be to the aura of New York City. That faraway place was France and her approach is like an impressionist's. But be assured that the details she has not elected to put down are nonetheless clearly and firmly in her mind, and that to seek to dissuade her about the validity of her interpretation is to court a most beautiful, delightful defeat. Her sisters-in-law grew up in Kentucky, far from France; nevertheless, mindful of the great French photographer, we often called them Miss Cartier and Miss Bresson, faithful recorders as they were of hundreds of decisive moments. It was traumatic to omit any of those moments here. One photographer we know claims he can tell which photographs are by one sister and which by another. It is a mystery to us and we shall enjoy trying to find out.

If enough people want the Central Park that Mireille, Nancy, and Retta Johnston see, it will be like that, free of the things that do not need to happen in it, serving its own good public purpose just as St. Patrick's does a few blocks down Fifth Avenue.

The Johnstons urged that Miss Marianne Moore, who knows the purpose well, introduce their book; Mrs. Millar Graff, who helped bring this about, wrote another Sierra Club member: "I had the shimmering joy and shuddersome responsibility of squiring Marianne Moore around Central Park in preparation for her writing of the introduction. . . . Miss Moore in her tricorne is just slightly less conspicuous than Abraham Lincoln in his stovepipe. Lunch at the Fountain was as private as the Court of St. James—I think she secretly enjoyed the attention—and our slow walks in the park were a royal progress as strangers bowed and smiled and murmured her name. I got her safely back to her house, very tired, I'm afraid, but full of admiration for the park, especially the wild northern part."

There is genius behind what Miss Moore admires there, and what she and the Johnstons and the Sierra Club see in the park as a whole. It is Frederick Law Olmsted's. His concepts informed the club's founders and its beginnings in 1892. Long before that, recovering from the travail of redesigning Central Park, he traveled west (1863), and for several months lived near Yosemite Valley. And here, in the collective judgment of Hans Huth, the *Dictionary of American Biography*, and Daniel H. Burnham, was the right man in the right spot at the right time, the man who was transmuting park ideals into a living force, the man who painted "with lakes and wooded slopes; with lawns and banks and forest-covered hills; with mountainsides and ocean views."

No one was better prepared to help the first national park, Yosemite, come into being in 1864, when the United States ceded Yosemite Valley to California to protect the nation's interest. The Valley was ceded back for better protection in 1905. Seven years before the establishment of Yellowstone National Park, in a preliminary report on Yosemite that was lost for eighty years, he enunciated the national park idea. His prose may be that of a report, but the clarity of his thinking still serves Yosemite, or should serve it, and Yellowstone and all national parks, no matter where, and Central Park too:

"The first point to be kept in mind then is the preservation and maintenance as exactly as is possible of the natural scenery; the restriction, that is to say, within the narrowest limits consistent with the necessary accommodation of visitors, of all artificial constructions and the prevention of all constructions markedly inharmonious with the scenery or which would unnecessarily obscure, distort, or detract from the dignity of the scene. . . . It is important that it be remembered that in permitting the sacrifice of anything that would be of the slightest value to future visitors to the convenience, bad taste, playfulness, carelessness, or wanton destructiveness of present visitors, we probably yield in each case the interest of uncounted millions to the selfishness of a few.''

What Ansel Adams calls ''the noble gestures of the natural world'' have no better protection than the national park idea, which recognizes that a park is for people, but especially for the people who like what the park is, who are content to wonder at what has always been beautiful and leave it that way.

In Central Park the beginnings of an understanding of other parks can happen. If so crowded an island can set aside so extensive an area, then communities everywhere should take heart. Central Park, with its introduction to greens and fragrance, helps people of a constricted city to sense what lies beyond the wall. It is fair to suggest that their devotion to the park has led Manhattan voters to defeat such schemes as the one to put a Panther Mountain dam in the Adirondack Forest Preserve. Most of the voters never had seen the preserve and probably never would, but they voted 3½ to 1 to defeat the dam.

Joseph W. Penfold, Conservation Director of the Izaak Walton League, proposed to an early Sierra Club Wilderness Conference in San Francisco that a map of the United States should be drawn in isoprims, lines showing the contour of primitiveness, even as isobars depict the contour of barometric pressure. No one has drawn that map yet, and someone should. The highs of primitiveness would be the two places in the lower forty-eight states that are more than ten miles from a road. The lows would be in any of several ghettos or slurbs. In New York City, Isoprim Zero is probably somewhere in Harlem. If it is indeed there, the situation may one day be corrected by some of the very people photographed here by the Johnstons, people from the man-made jungle who have learned about the man-made garden, where contours of primitiveness are emerging again. Here, however faintly, one can indeed hear the music the natural world has always danced to.

The Sierra Club's gratitude goes first to the Johnstons who had the idea for this book, who have loved Central Park for what it is and can be. If their work will help others see more clearly the beauty they have seen, and if these others wish it so, then Central Park will be enhanced. We are grateful for Marianne Moore's appreciation of the place; New York's poet laureate is a strong ally. We thank all the people who have manned the Central Park defenses, staving off proposals for inappropriate structures that would otherwise have used up the park's open space about three times in the last century. We thank them for our chance to know all the park's value and even how much it adds to the tax rolls, mindful of the cost of clearing alien buildings and putting the trees and sky back if the defenders had ever lost courage. We are glad we could help defend Central Park before various city administrators and in the courts. Our members and friends are ready to do it again but hope they will not need to.

We are pleased that Central Park is as big and complete as it is, and wish there could be more of it. We know especially how easy it would be to diminish it without reducing it, as Paul Brooks made clear in *The Atlantic Monthly:* ''The space available. . . . is not big enough for all who want to use it. But the size of the park is directly related to the manner in which you use it. If you are in a canoe traveling at three miles an hour, the lake on which you are paddling is ten times as long and ten times as broad as it is to the man in a speedboat going thirty. An hour's paddle will take you as far away as an hour in a speedboat—if there are no speedboats. In other words, more people can use the same space with the same results . . . every road that replaces a canoe paddle, shrinks the area of the park.''

So we are grateful, finally, for the special days each week when Central Park is bigger inside because Thomas Hoving asked automobiles to stay outside. After all, the human foot is a cleverly constructed device, amazingly efficient, and still capable of the direct contact that rewards those who will take time to feel the touch of the earth.

DAVID BROWER

San Francisco, September 9, 1968

INTRODUCTION

As early as 1836, William Cullen Bryant said in the *New York Evening Post* that the City of New York should reserve our forest and woodland for shade and refreshment as a park. He recalled that "at the beginning of the Century, anyone had been able to walk in half an hour from his home to the open fields that soon would be covered with brick and mortar." In London a year later than his original suggestion, Bryant requested for a park "a central reservation in New York" and today, we have that very thing, designed by Frederick Law Olmsted and Calvert Vaux, keeping Bryant's original words, Central Park.

As one comes down Fifth Avenue in early May, the air itself seems a delicate green by reason of the multitude of tiny leaves that appear to have come out overnight. Entering the park at 72d Street, one pauses to admire the ancient, small-leafed Chinese elm, one of the original planting, the largest Chinese elm in America. Just ahead, we have an example of Frederick Olmsted's genius; he makes the path turn so that as one looks back, one has lost the city and sees only a mass of green: lindens, oaks, elms and maples.

From the terrace above the Bethesda Fountain, one descends the wide steps, pausing for a moment to examine the accurately realized, square-framed, sculptured subjects, such as pears or a lotus pod, dogwood blossoms and a bird about to pick up a worm (a rather large worm lest it be overlooked). On the left, a tree towers over the stairway, a tall paulownia, or is it a catalpa? One notices then that the angel hovering over the pool is really hovering, without touching the water. A bird lights on her wing. One may catch the scent of mowed grass and see boats emerge from under Bow Bridge, which rises to an ellipse at the center that no oarsman need scrape the underside. This bridge is faded by weather to an ideal Oriental bleached blue.

Crossing Bow Bridge, of broad pale timbers, one comes to a wilder area —
masses of rock showing striations of the glacier, and in what direction the
mass moved. Roots of large trees clasp the rocks of the moraine, forming a
passage for water trickling down. At some places, brush has intentionally
been left for songbirds and one is startled by the note of a titmouse,
''Peter? Peter? Peter?'' A step farther, one hears the sound of a waterfall.

Near 100th Street and Central Park West, there are Osage oranges and a
bald cypress and sweetgum trees with a leaf that is deeper cut than a maple's.
On the hillside are towering tulip trees worthy of study. The smooth shaft
of the trunk rises like a column of steel. If it is spring, as the eye turns up
it catches the brilliance of flowers, greenish yellow and orange. A petal falls,
lending excitement when examined. Benches can be found along the walk,
and lamp posts designed by Henry Bacon, the post rising from a stylized
vine at the base.

Spring: masses of bloom, white and pink cherry blossoms on trees given
us by Japan. Summer: fragrance of black locust and yellow-wood flowers.
Autumn: a leaf rustles. Winter: one catches sight of a skater, arms folded,
leaning to the wind—the very symbol of peaceful solitude, of unimpaired
freedom. We talk of peace. This is it.

MARIANNE MOORE

New York City, July 20, 1968

1. CENTRAL PARK;

PROVINCE OF EVERY DREAM

The park is where the real and the possible cease to be contradictory.

Limits of time and space can be disregarded; routines and reticences
can be laid aside.

The variety offered by the city seems enormous but in fact is reserved to a few. For the others, the world remains on display but out of reach.

Disenchantment and despair prevail. The chance to experience the unexpected is lost to habit, regulation, and the oppressive maze.

Each who enters the park, leaving behind the limits of the familiar, is suddenly all-powerful and all-extraordinary.

We can break loose, leap right or left, attempt the impossible.
Impatience and zest take over. All joy is back.

All is available to everyone, in a universe that calls for happy boldness, that waits to give, to take, and to multiply the abundance brought to it.

Will you, won't you,
Will you, won't you,
Will you join the dance?

I can be a giant, a tree, a skyscraper, a hill.

I can fly the highest

[35

I can float and sail away. I can discover continents.

I count the drops of water, I can keep them in my hands.
I can find new friends.

I can transform the world.

I can learn anything I want—to dance, to sing, to grow.
When I get too tired to walk, I lie in the grass and become a pebble.

I can run in the snow. I can bark and jump
and snap at the white dust on the wing. I can become a wolf.

What else do I want to be?

What else do I want to do?

Each step leads to surprise and delight.
Exuberance spreads in this radiant province.

Dreams are celebrated until they yield to contented abandon.

The Professional Papers

There are places on the island easily accessible, and possessing all the advantages of wood, lawn and water, which might, at a comparatively small expense, be converted into a park, which would be at once the pride and ornament of the city. Such a park, well laid out, would become the favorite resort of all classes. There are thousands who pass the day of rest among the idle and dissolute, in porter-houses, or in places more objectionable, who would rejoice in being enabled to breathe the pure air in such a place, while the ride and drive through its avenues, free from the noise, dust and confusion inseparable from all thoroughfares, would hold out strong inducements for the affluent to make it a place of resort. [Mayor Ambrose C. Kingsland in his message of April 5, 1851 to the Common Council of the City of New York, quoted p. 25.]

The Park throughout is a single work of art, and as such subject to the primary law of every work of art, namely, that it shall be framed upon a single, noble motive, to which the design of all its parts, in some more or less subtle way, shall be confluent and helpful.

To find such a general motive of design for the Central Park, it will be necessary to go back to the beginning and ask, for what worthy purpose could the city be required to take out and keep excluded from the field of ordinary urban improvements, a body of land in what was looked forward to as its very centre, so large as that assigned for the Park? For what such object of great prospective importance would a smaller body of land not have been adequate?

To these questions a sufficient answer can, we believe, be found in the expectation that the whole of the island of New York would, but for such a reservation, before many years be occupied by buildings and paved streets; that millions upon millions of men were to live their lives upon this island, millions more to go out from it, or its immediate densely populated suburbs, only occasionally and at long intervals, and that all its inhabitants would assuredly suffer, in greater or less degree, according to their occupations and the degree of their confinement to it, from influences engendered by these conditions. [Pp. 248-249.]

The dominant and justifying purpose of Central Park was conceived to be that of permanently affording, in the densely populated central portion of an immense metropolis, a means to certain kinds of refreshment of the mind and nerves which most city dwellers greatly need and which they are known to derive in large measure from the enjoyment of suitable scenery. [P. 188.]

It is no exaggeration to say that this work is doing much towards elevating the general public taste of the country, not only in the more extended and spacious public and private dwellings and gardens, but in the adornment of the more numerous and less pretentious habitations of our rural population. [Annual Report of the Central Park Commissioners, 1863, quoted p. 176.]

It is a very general complaint that there is not in this great city, nor in its environs, any one proper spot, where its numerous inhabitants can enjoy, with convenience, the exercise that is necessary for health and amusement. [Letter in the New York Packet, August 15, 1785, quoted p. 18.]

Amusements and active play adapted for children were a constant concern. They were sought mainly through means directly contributing to the pleasant qualities of the landscape for others, or at worst neutral in their effect on the landscape,—means which would introduce pleasant kinds of animation without seriously impairing verdurousness or other desired landscape qualities. Subject only to such limitations as might prove necessary from time to time in various places for the general maintenance of verdurousness, the use of the lawns by children and especially by the smaller children whose wear and tear on good turf is much less than that of older children and adults, was to be encouraged and pro-

moted both for spontaneous unorganized play and for organized plays and pageantry. Numerous special devices, some long since fallen into disuse, were contrived for the special benefit of children, the buildings or other special equipment they involved being either woven harmoniously into the general fabric of the scenery or hidden away. [Pp. 195-196.]

[The designers of the Park sought] to adapt the physical design and construction of the Park as well as possible to its use by great numbers of people in a manner calculated to give the maximum of refreshing enjoyment without involving excessive wear and tear of a sort destructive to the scenic basis of that enjoyment. [P. 202.]

In one European public park we find a race-course, with its grand-stand, stables, pool-room, and betting ring; in another, popular diversions of the class which we elsewhere look to Barnum to provide. In one there is a theater with ballet-dancing; in another, soldiers firing field-pieces at a target, with a detail of cavalry to keep the public at a distance.

Attempts to introduce like provisions in several of our American parks have been resisted under the personal conviction that they would tend to subvert their more important purpose. In some of our parks, nevertheless, arrangements have been made for various games; concerts and shows have been admitted; there have been military parades; and it is impossible to find any line of principle between many favored and neglected propositions. [P. 531.]

The Park, as a whole, is undoubtedly expected to afford to the citizens of the metropolis, day after day and year after year, a succession of views of a rural character so real and genuine as to convey very positive ideas in regard to natural scenery, even to a person who might never see anything more country-like than will ultimately be contained within its limits; and this, in connection with the opportunity it offers for a social enjoyment of fresh air and exercise, is perhaps the most important service that it is calculated to perform in a direct way. Hill and dale, wood and water, grass and green leaves, are the natural food and refreshment of the human eye—an organ of sense [that is] so delicately adjusted as to require something more than dull and uninteresting forms, and is but little ministered to, in a pleasant way, in the portion of the city devoted to plain, straight-forward business or even domestic routine. [Central Park Commissioners, 1866, quoted p. 175.]

For example, rock has been removed, drains laid, deep soil formed and fine, short greens-ward gradually established upon the soil in certain places in order to secure that particular form of gratification which may be produced by a rich color and texture of turf, and by the contrast of this color and texture with that of other associated objects. To a limited extent and under certain conditions, the turf may be trodden upon without injury, but if walking upon it were generally allowed the particular object for which much labor during many years has been thus expended would be wholly lost. Hence it is an imperative part of the business of the Commissioners to prevent this misuse of it. . . .

Similar illustrations might be multiplied by the hundred, and keepers must realize that every foot of the Park's surface, every tree and bush, as well as every arch, roadway and walk has been fixed where it it is with a purpose, and upon its being so used that it may continue to serve that purpose to the best advantage, and upon its not being otherwise used, depends its value. . . . [P. 100.]

What artist so noble as he, who, with far-reaching conception of beauty and designing-power, sketches the outlines, writes the colors, and directs the shadows, of a picture so great that Nature shall be employed upon it for generations, before the work he has arranged for her shall realize his intentions! [P. 144.]

Frederick Law Olmsted, Sr.

2. NATURE AND CENTRAL PARK

"Le démenti des fleurs au vent de la panique."

—Aragon

Cities are made by men led by a dream, by their idea of beauty and their sense of purpose. Buildings, avenues, and monuments reflect the attempt to be faithful to the dream.

In New York, archetype of the modern city, the builders often seem to have abandoned the dream, to have lost all desire to seek either form or function; they seem to have resigned themselves to a city molded by forces they cannot try to foresee or modify.

Constricted by a proliferation of buildings, stupefied by the plethora of signs, glutted with traffic, deafened by engines, horns, sirens, and jackhammers, smothering in foul air, New York lives on its narrow island in a constant state of emergency.

It is the city of restlessness. Impatient to consume and cast aside, constantly on the move, hurriedly built and compulsively destroyed, New York remains forever unfinished.

Central Park proposes new alternatives: the serenity of a cluster
of trees, the softness of pebbles and grass in the sun, the radiance of a
shivering pond, the truce.

Nature in the park is not quite wild. The basic rocks were modified, the ponds and reservoir built, the pavement laid, the grass, shrubs, and trees planted. The park was made to remind the city of what it overwhelmed and might so easily forget. Central Park country is a created country in which man seeks to restore nature, to recreate the openness and diversity of real countryside, and to free the forces of renewal.

Central Park offers no pastoral retreat from civilization. Instead it proposes a model of what all civilized communities might contain, of what New York should cling to.

In Paris the magnificently open boulevards, the trim gardens, the elaborate monuments offer a rational and coherent universe, totally intelligible to man, which, mellowed by time, keeps modifying the present with the evidence of the past. In New York what is not immediately relevant and functional is rejected, and so the New Yorker is forever a stranger in his city. Landmarks pass and each generation is cut off from its own past. The city is not a museum; it briefly records man's achievements and celebrates his current deeds. And where Paris and her gardens symbolize French identity, French past, French dreams, New York represents the evanescent in the American adventure.

The city and the park mirror each other, offer a counterpoint to each other, reflect a truth that is peculiarly theirs, and only theirs. Both present dazzling variety. The architecture of the city displays a startling potpourri of shapes and styles—Gothic spires, aggressive glass buildings, Georgian brick houses. The city's juxtaposition of grandeur, quaint shabbiness, efficiency, and waste can be matched by the civilized variety of the park's narrow paths, formal terraces, playfields, romantic stone bridges, improbable statues, and pervasive intrusions. In the park the diversity of the city finds its complement.

Both the park and the city have outgrown their original designs, and both have to meet new needs to maintain their vitality.

The city is a dynamic, evergrowing universe, striving to grow higher and spread farther. The wrecking ball swings on the old low buildings to make room for new higher ones. And just as insistently new plans are proposed to take from the park—which can no longer spread and could never grow higher—those elements the park provides the city and that the city needs to pursue its quest for grace and beauty: diversity, air, light, open space, tangible harmonies.

There is no sharp emphasis in Central Park, no excess in proportion, no insistent order. Everywhere a gentle, delicate variety of forms. The surface of the ground is subtly revealed by ponds with irregular shores, by lanes that wind and climb, by small hills that roll gently or plunge sharply. The juxtapositions of rocks and planting are so carefully arranged that nowhere in the park can one sense its full size or shape. Each path reveals a new sequence of light, color, pattern, and fragrance.

All is present and speaks of what is here now.
All is present and summons me to be all here.
Not dreaming, comparing, longing, but here,
totally given to the moment.
I know the tonic of being without questioning.
From this confidence in the moment comes my joy.
I decipher the dancing shades on the water,
the intricate shimmer of its surface.
There is so much for me to learn
from the grace and abandon of a blossom,
the languor of a warm afternoon sky,
the meditation of a pigeon by the lake.
Each tree is here for me to discover,
each a miracle of gratuitous exuberance,
a festival of movements and colors
linking earth and melting clouds.
Textured rocks, gently sloping meadows,
frail grass shivering in the light.
I can take an endless inventory of gifts.

The pond is alive; the thousand little suns sparkling in it are scattered by the wind and a thousand more take their place.

The sky is not that of the city, shredded by the peaks of the tall buildings that hold it up. Instead, it is a vast, mobile, luminous foam, turning softer and paler as it nears the horizon.

The light seizes all the shapes and enflames them. It creates new objects, stresses new lines, discovers and outlines secret shadows. Ceaselessly it unveils a skein of changing forms and patterns.

The jostling and din are remote now, and the frenzy of owning, the stifling of initiative that lulls the senses and weakens élan.

To share the park's grace and vitality one learns new gestures, perceives in a new way. It is a clumsy, awkward time, a time of patience and gentleness. The rhythm of the earth is slow and one must be attentive.

Change me sun, transform me, too,
make me look as new as I feel inside.
You give me so much to see,
you varnish the bark, the leaf, the rock;
make me shining and glowing too.
I discover time for abandon, for lazy meditation,
for the delight of feeling so helpless
and heavy under the sun.
I enjoy at leisure, chin on my hand,
the quality of silence, the quality of light.
The grass stops my sight and my thoughts wander
in soft clouds that expand, fly, and vanish.
Detached, I can at last be all to myself.
This plenitude of impressions,
I absorb and taste with new senses.
I discover verve and tenacity.
I see the separateness of all things,
I perceive a fresh world
in which nothing is to be taken for granted.

The stripes, the pleats, the scratches in the rock speak of former changes and violence. The texture of the meadows, the shapes of trees, tell of the force of the winds and the rains.

No matter how dry or scorching the summer, how bitter the winter, how ruthless the wave of cold, the park always manages to keep alive its generous share of miracles: a fragile March violet, rusted by the cold, tentative in a patch of yellow grass, a baby pigeon trying its first flight from the dry branch of a tree, a pale crocus piercing the brown melting snow, a bud stretching toward sunlight. These things speak of ingenuity, of endurance, of difficulties overcome. This is a fragile and touching nature, scarred hills, frail grass, ragged meadows, trampled lanes—never the opulent nature of the wilderness.

It is a nature that knows suffering. These hills, these ponds and fields, these benches are the refuge for the forgotten, the poor, the lonely, the sad, the old and wounded. It is their haven, protected from the strident noises of the streets.

They may not fit in any race. They may be shy and vulnerable. For their grief, their memories, their hopes, for their being alive, here they do not have to apologize. Here they have their place. They are not strangers in it.

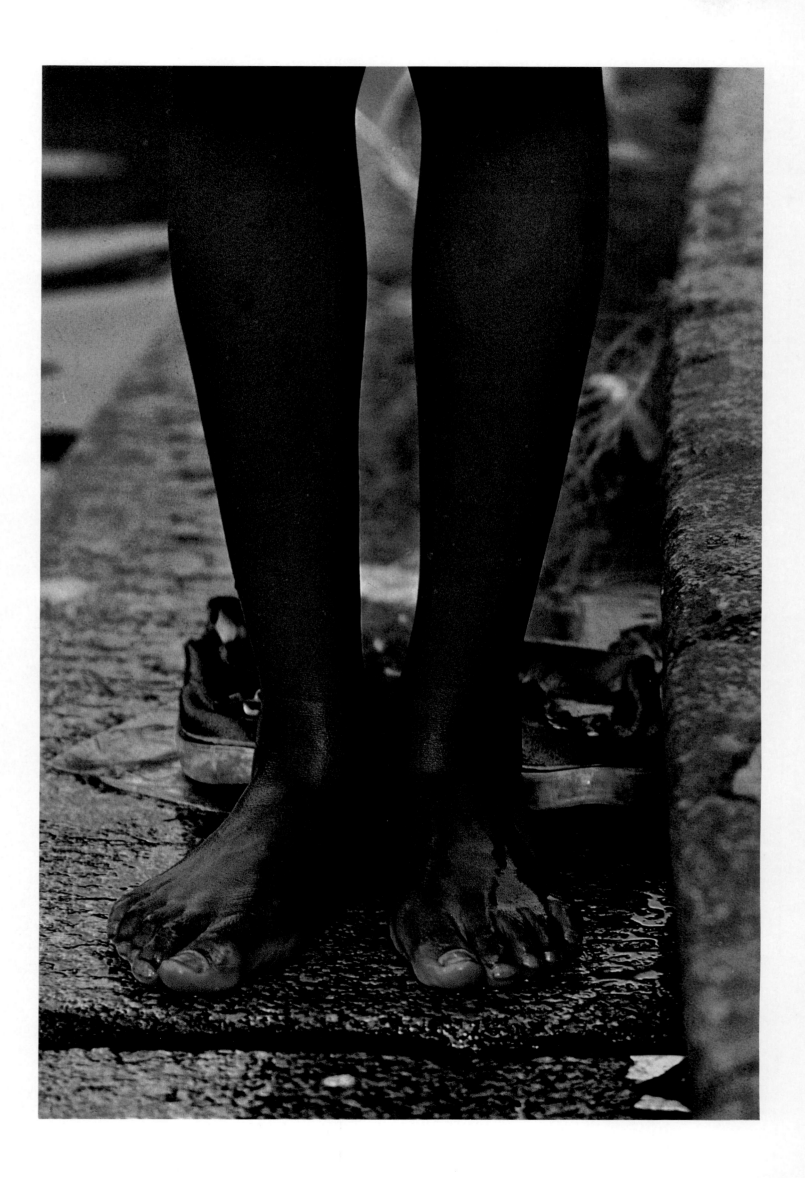

What a comforting love.
This pigeon I feed needs me,
watches me, waits for me.
I can stop twenty times,
dream a little, rest a little, move about,
walk by the pond, lie on the grass,
perceive the wonder of a squirrel,
industrious, gracefully busy, its ears pointed delicately,
its hair iridescent in the sun.

There is peace, there is leisure, there are precious encounters.

Days linger in the park. The narrow lanes have a life of their own, and lead to special territories —and to special tranquility. In the city we are too caught up, too feverish in work and pleasures to evaluate our place, our roles, in serenity. The trepidation, the incessant solicitation, the anxiety, the proliferation of experiences make us apathetic; our constantly provoked desires are frustrated.

Limited to the pursuit of set aims, we live so constantly on the *qui vive* that we are no longer alert. We must be still. In the park, we are at last able to recollect, to renew our dreams, to take time to decipher them.

On the grass, on the lake, nature does not impose on me,
does not intrude, does not try to direct me.
I can be oblivious if I wish; I can be calm;
I can savor the fragile and delicious moment.
I can sit in the center of myself,
I slowly coincide with myself, at last.

I learn to respect some mysteries, to understand indecision,
to permit hesitation, to enjoy gratuitous impulses,
to taste life without trying to understand all its meaning.
I am delivered from the need to produce, to manage, to grasp.
I perceive new equations between things and people.
I have time to clarify half-dreamed visions within me.
The sky which seemed so much to bear down on me
recedes here; the air is light and ample.
The inexhaustible energy of the park
makes me feel stronger, richer, barer.
I have new eyes, new ears,
and time to use them.

The Professional Papers

The main popular want to be ministered to in a large park situated like the Central Park, with respect to a great city, is the natural craving of its residents for opportunity to exercise a variety of capacities for enjoyment which must necessarily remain unused, and through disuse tend to feebleness or distortion under the ordinary limitations of a city experience, however rich this may be in other respects. Three things should be supplied in a park not to be had in the city elsewhere: First, air, purified by abundant foliage. Second, means of tranquilizing and invigorating exercise, as in good quiet roads and walks, kept free from the irritating embarrassments of the city streets. Third, extended landscapes, to refresh and delight the eye, and, therefore, as free as possible from the rigidity and confinement of the city and from the incessant emphasis of artificial objects which inevitably belong to its ordinary conditions. [P. 489.]

There is also another space of ground, which calls loudly for the hand of improvement— now a public nuisance, from whence the inhabitants of the neighborhood are infested, during the summer season, with continual clouds of stinking dust, if not as pestiferous as the heated sands of the desert Arabia, yet sufficiently obnoxious, to demand immediate attention from those, who have the means of remedying the evil in their power. The ground I mean is the place commonly called the Fields.—This place laid out with judgment and taste, would become a blessing to the inhabitants of New York, and an elegant ornament to a fine city. [P. 19.]

In that area there would be space enough to have broad reaches of park and pleasure-grounds, with a real feeling of the breadth and beauty of green fields, the perfume and freshness of nature. In its midst would be located the great distributing reservoirs of the Croton aqueduct, formed into lovely lakes of limpid water, covering many acres, and heightening the charm of the sylvan accessories by the finest natural contrast. In such a park, the citizens who would take excursions in carriages, or on horseback, could have the substantial delights of country roads and country scenery, and forget for a time the rattle of the pavements and the glare of brick walls. Pedestrians would find quiet and secluded walks when they wished to be solitary, and broad alleys filled with thousands of happy faces, when they would be gay. The thoughtful denizen of the town would go out there in the morning to hold converse with the whispering trees, and the wearied tradesmen in the evening, to enjoy an hour of happiness by mingling in the open spaces with "all the world." [Andrew Jackson Downing in the Horticulturist, August 1851, quoted p. 27.]

Provisions for the improvement of the ground, however, pointed to something more than mere exemption from urban conditions, namely, to the formation of an opposite class of conditions; conditions remedial of the influences of urban conditions.
Two classes of improvements were to be planned for this purpose; one directed to secure pure and wholesome air, to act through the lungs; the other to secure an antithesis of objects of vision to those of the streets and houses. . . . [P. 45.]

The Park is an enclosed ground devoted to such popular amusements as can, with proper regard to the convenience and pleasure of the general public, be enjoyed in the open air.
This area is situated in the centre of the city, having a population not altogether homogeneous, reared in different climes, and bringing to the society of the metropolis views of

labor and ideas of social enjoyment differing as widely as the temperature of the various countries of their origin. A day's work in the large cities of Europe, and a day's work in New York, are not the same; the amusements and routine of the daily life of the Sicilian and Scotchman are dissimilar. Each brings with him the traditions and the habits of his own country. The work of fusing the people of differing nationalities into a homogeneous body can be accomplished only during the life of two or three generations, and it would be difficult to prescribe rules that would satisfy these dissimilar tastes and habits.

The most that can be attained at the Park, is to afford an opportunity for those recreations or entertainments that are generally acceptable, and to exclude such as will, though perhaps acceptable to a considerable number, in practice impair the attractions of a common place of recreation to such larger numbers.

It is daily observation, that individuals, even of the same nationality, reared in the same city, have, by reasons of difference in education or from other circumstances, acquired habits so diverse as to render the entertainments that afford gratification to one unsuitable to another.

There is, however, a universality in nature, that affords a field of enjoyment to all observers of her works. [Central Park Commissioners, 1863, quoted p. 407.]

Frederick Law Olmsted, Sr.

Subject to somewhat closer limitations as to intensity and continuity of use, in order to avoid serious destruction of the verdurousness of the greater park landscapes, a considerable amount of baseball and other active games by older boys and youths was one of the by-products definitely expected to result from the large open meadows designed primarily for scenic enjoyment and obtainable on the difficult rocky terrain of Central Park only at great expense,—a by-product desirable not only for the youths engaging in it but for the larger public enjoying the animated but verdurous and refreshing scene.

It was quite deliberately concluded that with a population as large as would become tributary to Central Park it was wholly impossible to make provision in it for the entire youthful part of that population to enjoy continuously as much as they might like of baseball playing or other active sports involving hard wear and tear on the ground surface, or to make provision for a large amount of space per capita, without radically subordinating to those ends the dominant scenic purpose of the Park. It was thought inevitable in some cases and expedient in others to provide within the Park boundaries for some other objectives, involving conditions equally incompatible with the scenic qualities proper to the Park, by the process of excision; by deliberately withdrawing certain areas from the landscape of the Park, and using them for these other objectives. In this class were the transverse roads, the widenings of boundary streets, the reservoirs, some service buildings, the carousel, and the site of the Metropolitan Museum of Art. Large areas of bare ground or shabbily worn-out turf, inevitable where active athletic games are constantly played, differ from all of the above except the reservoirs in their extent, and differ from all except the Museum in the absence of any strong logical reason for their location within the boundaries of Central Park. If it had been considered a legitimate charge upon the funds of the Central Park Commission to provide such un-parklike fields for intensive play, the million dollars spent for extending the original area of the Park northward to 110th Street would logically have been spent in acquiring several separate play fields in adjacent parts of Manhattan, where each would have been closely surrounded by the population it was to serve and would have caused less interruption of the street system. [Pp. 196-197.]

3. GAMES

Football, chess, hockey, soccer—we can at last elect our challenges. Liberated from a world where reward and necessity dictate all activities, we play the games, submitting freely to their aims, their rules, their pace.

For now a power, diverse and equal for each participant, is offered; vigor and discipline are asked in return.

Discarding ease, we seek resistances to win over. In the expansive atmosphere of the field, a hunter, a warrior, a strategist emerges.

Some show their grace, their strength, their craft; others observe and applaud. Spectator and participant, we are one in the same adventure. We share dangers, victories, and defeats with equal fervor.

Enhancing the cohesion and the uniqueness of the group, we bring badges, uniforms, flags, and songs with us.

Making choices, taking risks, measuring skills, being tested—these become gratuitous joys. We are intoxicated with activity, with the moment. The explosion of vitality is not escape from reality but excursion into it.

In this chosen frame, the struggles, the tensions, the forces out of which
the city life is made are contained, transmuted by the game into elements
of a clear and chosen deed, a happy trial.

Repetitive city tasks imposed on us have left us dull, immobilized between the poles of apathy and outrage, slow to initiate or direct the course of our lives.

In the park the games people play are a liberation, even if only for a while; the cohesion and the warmth they yield is lasting.

Tomorrow, fragmentation and ambiguity will return; but diminished by the boldness and confidence of this passionate participation, this exhilaration of the heart, of the senses, of the mind.

The limited, definite, visible endeavor offers a limited, definite, visible result—a satisfaction, with more elation in victory and less in defeat, but satisfaction just the same.

From the Professional Papers
of Frederick Law Olmsted, Sr.

Two other secondary aspects of the Park's functions which the designers stressed were those of affording what they called family pleasures and gregarious pleasures. Except for a few conveniences, in part long since abandoned, that were especially adapted for the convenience of family picnic parties, and the deliberately close association of facilities for little children's amusement with places pleasant for their parents, the former was not specifically expressed in the physical plan of the Park but rather in plans for its administration and for the education of the public in its most effective use. Regard for gregarious pleasures was constantly present in considering all users of the Park as forming the animated part of its scenery, in the manipulation of walks and roads and bridle paths so as to afford to a high degree in certain places the pleasure of seeing throngs of others in holiday mood, while in other places securing a sense of retirement from crowds. In the Mall and Terrace the most specific attempt was made to provide for concentrated gregarious enjoyment, enlivened by music, and in a frankly formal landscape setting considered peculiarly appropriate to that gregarious mood. [P. 197.]

4. PARADE

There is little time for idling, observing, sharing in New York. In shops, by drugstore counters, at newsstands, people meet, but the contacts remain transactions. People are background, they walk, drive, speak faster and faster, as if to negate other presences. Few stop long enough to see, to hear, or to know others. The main concern is to avoid being in each other's way, to get by, to survive. Violence, indifference, and speed bruise all possible encounters. In the irritated noisy flow of cars and in the near-collisions of pedestrians, so much is never noticed, never uttered, never heard.

With no common faith, isolated, alone, we and our ignorances coexist and the solitudes are crueler than elsewhere. Yet cities were born from a need for exchange, evaluation, challenge. One brings his dreams to the city to be tested, to be shared.

All kinds of visitors come to the park, and each has his own entrance; there is the artist's gate, the scholar's gate, the farmer's gate, the warrior's gate, even the stranger's gate—gates enough to let the largest, most diverse society find its way in.

To the park New Yorkers bring the images they propose of themselves.
The fragmented, dispersed life acquires unity, beauty, and purpose.
Here they can share and, in sharing, together they can reinvent the world.
A stylized life begins and every day is Sunday.

In the park, between the limits of trees and hilly meadows, the light is right for discerning smiles and faces once again. The park is a crossroad designed for confrontation. The Fountain, the Ramble, Sheep Meadow are a core, a piazza, a forum for New Yorkers. The park is a place to separate individuals, where after being annoyed, awed, smothered by crowds, one can come to see and to be seen. It is a place in which to be unique and beautiful. Besides finding dignity, besides liberating ourselves from exclusion and routine, we come here to find our own grace. Fleeing loneliness, monotony, and the ordinary and predictable, we seek here new faces, new ways of being.

Here all is possible: we are outrageous, splendidly arrogant, disconcerting, flamboyant. And this deliberate new identity gives relevance and beauty to our existence. We do not seek total disguise: we simply assume the features of the person we want to be and in doing so gain delight and pride. Through chosen ornaments we construct this self. And every adornment carries significance and attests, "I am singular, I am different, I am worthy of full attention. I, I, I."

In the parade, the backdrop, the costumes, and the movements, are all on display and are equally revealing. Walking, being looked at, observing crystallizes new patterns, awakens new preoccupations. Surprised, curious, admiring glances are tokens, and, although the spectators are essential to the parade, their verdict is no more than the necessary imprimatur that confirms the new invented self. So we walk, we stroll, we stand strategically, we carefully evaluate the scene, we perform. Tweedy casualness, militarized elegance, Cleopatrian languor, disarming childishness: we are on display.

The unity of each costume, the precision of each detail, the grace of each new gesture expresses the chosen essence. This invented self is more convincing, more brilliant, more readable than any given one: it guides new attitudes, regulates new movements, defines new moods.

The Fountain, the Mall, the Zoo are arenas, battlefields, meeting grounds, galleries, where eyes take time to choose what to rest on, what to be amused or bewildered or charmed by.

Differences are not only acknowledged and voiced, but sought. Arab sheiks, tender Alices, Indian Princes, grave Ophelias, safari explorers, mingle with less imaginative paraders who seek only a partial metamorphosis.

There are so many differences to be affirmed. Generations rediscover each other. East Side nonchalance confronts West Side vitality. Teeny boppers move languidly under the appraising glance of aloof nannies. Caped and bearded hippies and the carefully casual surprise each other.

In the boats, on the pond, in picnics on the meadows, and strolls by the zoo, the parade blossoms.

Each parader evaluates, judges, ratifies the harmonies, the startling details, the composed balances. There is so much to be explained, so much to be guessed.

Even the reluctant residents take part in the parade.

Crowds gather to laugh and enjoy the odd inhabitants of the zoo. Threaded through their fascination are touches of pity and sadness. But to the children the captivity of the animals is neither apparent nor disturbing. They simply see new kinds of life, life in new shapes, and they are full of reverence and awe before it.

For the lovers, the park is a ground they discover all to themselves, where love can be tested, challenged, and made known. Lovers need a region in which love can flourish. They do not want to be dependent on time or events. They reject the ephemeral, the given, the predictable. In this temple of shades and greenery, under the detached scrutiny of the statues, near the active ebullience of the squirrels, of the pigeons, and the sparrows, lovers celebrate their special mass.

Walking, pausing, they repeat as if it were a litany their new discovery: "We met. We touched. We love."

There is room for quiet, sensible love, for grave passionate love, and for cheerful lighthearted love. There is room for dreamy, tender, timid love, and for foolish whimsical love.

The lovers glorify love as a festivity, a ritual, a dance.

And in the parade strolling in the park, in the secret smiles of the lovers, in the amused, speculative, and tender glances of the passers-by, the boldness of the paraders forms a fluid society in which life is one with open delight.

But some of the strange characters here are inhabitants, permanently scattered throughout the park. They are the sober statues. There are few dancing satyrs and no languid nymphs or naked gods in Central Park, but a disconcerting gathering of brown, white, and golden statues, in varied patina, all solemn and exemplary, to remind us of human discoveries, human victories, and human dreams.

On the Mall a thoughtful Shakespeare faces a bewildered Columbus, who stands flag in hand, thankful eyes toward the sky, forever gazing at the discovered shores. Beyond him a Pilgrim father, leaning on his rifle, remains serene under the cluster of sleepy pigeons that stroll all over him. Farther on, the light through the branches of the trees leaves strange tattoos on Walter Scott.

Alice, stubborn and curious, sits on her enormous mushroom. Beside her the White Rabbit, frozen in eternal haste, holds his rusty watch. The more adventurous children nest on the rabbit's head; the more timid hide under the small mushrooms.

Hans Andersen, pensive, long-nosed, watches the sailing boats on the conservatory pond while young explorers crawl over his book and his top hat, rest on his knees, or sit by his friendly duck. Near by are the heroes of the First World War, their fingers glued in salute, their eyes fixed in perpetual victory.

Accompanied though the statues are by the familiar accessory —gun, book, flag—magical force emerges from them. They seem to acquire a life of their own. They welcome dead leaves, lost balloons, adventurous children, sleepy pigeons, busy squirrels. Their stone and metal show no scars. They never cry, nor fear nor doubt nor fret, nor run. Emancipated from time, snug under snow in winter, glistening in the showers of spring, warm in the sun, mysterious in lamplight, they glorify human myths.

And walking among them in this drafty museum, the visitors find their own myths and live them.

The parade frees images; it intensifies perception, energy, and direction; it expands dreams. This vibrant society, flowing under the trees, acquires a flamboyant fullness and finds joy in being part of a chosen world. Reality is purified and refined. The humblest element acquires its own luminous quality. A picnic, a boat ride, an encounter is transmuted.

The parade in the park illuminates the diversity of life and improvises
a richer one.

   Subtly altered, we return to the city, enhanced.